CHECK FOR CD-ROM

WOEIC

™

AQA

Self Study Guide

Clare Parker

OXFORD
UNIVERSITY PRESS

OXFORD
UNIVERSITY PRESS

Great Clarendon Street, Oxford OX2 6DP

Oxford University Press is a department of the University of Oxford.
It furthers the University's objective of excellence in research, scholarship,
and education by publishing worldwide in

Oxford   New York
Auckland   Cape Town   Dar es Salaam   Hong Kong   Karachi
Kuala Lumpur   Madrid   Melbourne   Mexico City   Nairobi
New Delhi   Shanghai   Taipei   Toronto

With offices in

Argentina   Austria   Brazil   Chile   Czech Republic   France   Greece
Guatemala   Hungary   Italy   Japan   South Korea   Poland   Portugal
Singapore   Switzerland   Thailand   Turkey   Ukraine   Vietnam

Oxford is a registered trade mark of Oxford University Press
in the UK and in certain other countries

British Library Cataloguing in Publication Data

Data available

ISBN 978-0-19 -915403-6

1 3 5 7 9 10 8 6 4 2

Typeset by PDQ Digital Media Solutions Ltd.
Printed in Great Britain by Ashford Colour Press Ltd.

Acknowledgements

The author and publisher would like to thank Melissa Weir (project
manager), Deborah Manning (editor), and Marion Dill (language
consultant).

Contents

Here's a reminder of the topics from the AQA A2 specification which you need to revise for the examination. You have to study the first three topics and must also choose two cultural topics.

Environment

Pollution – Energy – Protecting the planet

The Multicultural Society

Immigration – Integration – Racism

Contemporary Social Issues

Wealth and poverty – Law and order – Impact of scientific and technological progress

Cultural topics (two must be studied)

A region of Germany, Austria or German-speaking Switzerland

A period of 20th century history in Germany or a German-speaking country

The work of an author writing in German

The work of a dramatist or poet writing in German

The work of a director, architect, musician or painter from a German-speaking community

You will be taking two examinations:

Unit 3: Listening, Reading and Writing

This paper is worth 35% of your A Level and the time allowed is two hours and thirty minutes. There are three sections:

Listening – Reading and Writing – Writing

Unit 4: Speaking Test

The Speaking Test is worth 15% of your A Level. The test lasts 15 minutes and you have 20 minutes to prepare beforehand. You are not allowed to use a dictionary. There are two sections:

Discussing a stimulus card (5 minutes)

General conversation on topics you have studied (10 minutes)

Remember that your AS grade represents 50% of your A Level.

Pass grades for this examination range from A* and A down to E.

The descriptions of what you need to be able to do are very similar to those at AS Level, **but remember that this is in the context of the more demanding texts and tasks which you will meet at A2.** Two new things which are expected are an ability to translate from and into German accurately and an ability to cope with the unpredictable when you are talking to someone. Here's a reminder of the other expectations:

If you pass A Level German with an A grade, it means you can:

▶ clearly understand spoken language, including details and opinions.

▶ work out what someone is trying to say even if they don't spell it out in detail.

▶ clearly understand written texts, understanding both the gist and the details.

▶ talk fluently, giving your opinions and justifying them, and using a good range of vocabulary and generally accurate pronunciation and word order.

▶ organise your ideas and write them up well in German.

▶ write using a wide range of vocabulary and grammatical structures without making many mistakes.

If you pass A Level German with an E grade, it means you:

▶ show some understanding of spoken German, even if you have difficulties when the language is complex and miss some of the details.

▶ can sometimes work out what someone is trying to say even if they don't give all the details.

▶ understand straightforward written texts, although you don't always understand more difficult writing.

▶ can speak in German, and convey basic information, perhaps a little hesitantly and relying on material you have learned by heart. There is probably some English influence on your pronunciation.

▶ can convey information in writing, perhaps with some difficulty in organising your material and expressing it.

▶ use a range of vocabulary and structures, but quite often you make mistakes.

Preparing for the exams
You can see from these lists that when planning your revision there are really six areas you need to practise:

Speaking – Listening – Reading – Writing – Vocabulary – Grammar

There are tips on how to prepare each area overleaf.

Speaking

▶ Take every opportunity to practise speaking German – in lessons, with the language assistant, with a friend, with anyone you know who speaks German.

▶ Think up some controversial statements linked to each topic from the first three sections on page 4 and practise arguing for or against them. An example would be *‚Es ist verständlich, warum rechtradikale Parteien an Popularität gewinnen!‘*. Record your ideas on tape and listen to see what areas still need practice – perhaps fluency, pronunciation, word order or good use of vocabulary and structures.

▶ Think about all the aspects of the two cultural topics you have studied and practise explaining them and giving your opinions. Don't write everything out in full; note just a few key words down for reference, but definitely no full sentences.

Listening

▶ Keep listening to German, ideally every day. Use a mix of extracts you have worked on and new texts.

▶ Try listening to something for which you have the transcript. Just listen first, then listen again with the transcript and, if necessary, look up unknown words. Finally, listen again without the transcript and challenge yourself to understand everything.

▶ Watching films is excellent listening practice and watching more than once is even better! Try watching with the subtitles and then without. If you find this hard going, just re-watch a short extract.

▶ German radio and TV programmes are useful, but can also be difficult. Record an extract and listen or watch it more than once. You will find it gets easier.

▶ Try listening to some German songs without words and then with the words.

▶ Make sure you do some exam listening practice too!

Reading

▶ Keep reading a mix of things you read once quickly, such as a magazine, and things where you work hard at a short passage and try to understand everything. Texts from your textbook are useful for this.

▶ It's useful to note new vocabulary from your reading, but don't make it such hard work that you give up. Note, say, three new words from each text.

▶ Try a 'dual-language' reading book, where you get the original German on one page and an English translation on the opposite one. This is an excellent way to practise reading longer texts without losing heart!

▶ Read cartoons in German, such as "Calvin and Hobbes", "Garfield" or "Peanuts". These are very popular and easily available and can be very easily understood. (They are also very funny!)

▶ Search on the internet for articles in German on any topic which interests you.

Writing

▶ Write out the basic facts for each aspect of the cultural topics you have studied and learn them.

▶ Practise planning essay questions on your cultural topics, jotting down ideas for each paragraph – in German! – along with key vocabulary.

▶ Look carefully at marked work and identify what grammar errors you are making. Then look them up in a grammar book and try some practice exercises.

▶ Make sure you are writing – and learning! – lists of key vocabulary for each of the two cultural topics. In addition, learn a good range of 'essay phrases' for introducing ideas, giving opinions, summing up and so on.

Vocabulary

▶ Learn lists of words regularly and build in time to go back over words you learned a week or two ago. Reinforcement makes them stick!

▶ Choose a system of recording new words which works for you. It could be paper lists, sticky notes round the mirror, small sections on individual cards, index cards with German on one side and English meaning on the other, recording the German words and their English meanings on tape, making posters to stick on your bedroom wall ... what's important is that you are noting the words and going over them regularly!

▶ You were probably encouraged to use a good range of vocabulary in the essays you wrote during the year. Go back over them, highlighting good words and phrases and writing the English in the margin, then use this to test yourself. Words are often easier to learn in context.

Grammar

▶ Keep doing practice exercises in areas where you know you are weak.

▶ Use reading texts to practise thinking grammatically. For example, highlight a selection of adjectives, then write out the English for the phrases in which they appear. Test yourself by reproducing the German phrases accurately, complete with all the correct agreements!

▶ Keep thinking about word order. Analyse sentences regularly, looking at the position of the verb (past participle if appropriate). Is the **Time – Manner – Place** rule being applied at all times?

▶ Keep learning from your verb tables until you know all the forms of each tense of regular verbs and the most common irregular verbs. Test yourself using a die. 1 = *ich,* 2 = *du,* 3 = *er/sie/es,* 4 = *wir,* 5 = *ihr,* 6 = *sie/Sie.* Use a verb list, choose an infinitive and a tense at random, throw the die and say the correct form of the verb. Practise until you can do it without hesitation.

The Speaking Test: what you need to know

The test has two parts: discussing a stimulus card and a conversation on the two cultural topics you have studied.

Discussing a stimulus card (5 minutes)

▶ Choose one of the two cards you are given and spend the preparation time on it.

▶ Decide which of the two views expressed on the card you are going to defend and prepare an outline of your reasons which lasts no more than one minute.

▶ The examiner will challenge you to defend your point of view. Try to predict what arguments s/he might use and then plan how you will counter them.

▶ You are allowed to make notes. Don't write out exactly what you will say, but do note some useful vocabulary for the topic and some expressions for voicing your opinion and for disagreeing with someone.

To do well on this section you need to develop a wide range of relevant arguments to defend the viewpoint you have chosen. You must respond readily to the examiner's arguments and be able to counter them robustly, giving reasons for your views and reasons why you don't accept that the points s/he makes are justified.

Conversation (10 minutes)

You will be asked to spend about 5 minutes discussing each of the cultural topics you have studied, i.e. two of the following:

▶ a region
▶ a historical period
▶ an author
▶ a poet or dramatist
▶ a director, architect, musician or painter.

This section is marked on three aspects:

▶ **fluency**, which means speaking confidently and sustaining a conversation at a natural pace

▶ **interaction**, i.e. answering what you are asked, but also taking the opportunity to develop your ideas and to cope if the examiner contradicts you.

▶ **pronunciation** and **intonation**, which really means sounding as 'German' as possible.

In addition, both sections of the oral are marked for knowledge of grammar. You need to use a variety of structures and a good range of vocabulary, using correct word order, without making too many errors!

▶ Look at the card and read the two statements in the speech bubbles.

▶ Choose ONE and think how you can convey and expand on its main ideas.

▶ Begin the discussion by outlining your point of view (this should take no more than one minute).

▶ You must then be prepared to respond to anything the examiner might say and to justify your point of view.

▶ You may be required to explain something you have said, to respond to an opposing point of view expressed by the examiner, or to defend your expressed opinion(s).

▶ You may make notes in your preparation time and refer to them during this part of the examination.

Wie sollen wir die zukünftige Energiekrise lösen?

Es ist sehr wichtig, dass man weitere erneuerbare Energiequellen findet. Bald werden wir kein Öl mehr haben und wie wird dann alles weiter funktionieren?

Die einzige Lösung ist Atomenergie, weil sie sauber und preiswert ist. In der Zukunft werden wir sie immer mehr nötig haben.

This is **not** an exercise which requires you to balance both sides of an argument. Decide which of the two points of view you are going to defend, then stick to it! Come up with several reasons which support this viewpoint and be prepared to express them concisely in the opening section of the discussion.

Whichever side of the argument you choose to defend, the examiner will come up with reasons to challenge you. Prepare for this by writing a list of arguments s/he might use, then working out what you will say to counter each one. Look back at the speaking card on page 9, decide which side of the argument you are going to defend and write a list of tricky questions the examiner might ask. When you have done that, work out a good answer for each one. Then compare your ideas with those given upside down below.

Für die erneuerbare Energiequelle

Q: Glauben Sie, dass es realistisch ist, dass man die benötigte Energie von erneuerbaren Quellen bekommen kann?

A: Zur Zeit scheint es nicht sehr realistisch zu sein, aber mit Forschung und neuer Technologie wird es vielleicht in der Zukunft möglich sein. ...

Q: Wie kann man Autos mit Sonnen- und Windenergie betreiben?

A: Es gibt schon Autos, die mit Elektrizität fahren, und es ist also möglich, dass man weiterhin Fahrzeuge produziert, die von anderen Energiequellen betrieben werden.

Q: Unser Energiebedarf steigt immer mehr. Glauben Sie, dass es genug Energie geben wird, wenn wir uns nur auf erneuerbare Quellen verlassen?

A: Ich glaube, wir sollten unsere Einstellung ändern. Wir benutzen schon viel zu viel Energie, und wir müssen lernen, unseren Verbrauch einzuschränken. Wir könnten zum Beispiel ...

Für Atomenergie

Q: Finden Sie nicht, dass Atomenergie einfach sehr gefährlich ist? Wir leiden immer unter den Auswirkungen von Atomunfällen.

A: Ich denke schon, dass Atomenergie gefährlich ist, aber ich glaube, dass man jetzt viel mehr darüber weiß und ...

Q: Man hat noch nicht richtig entschieden, wie man Atommüll am besten beseitigen kann, also ist es nicht vernünftig, weitere Atomkraftwerke zu bauen, oder?

A: Ja, es gibt in mehreren Ländern schon Plätze für Atommüll, und man findet immer noch neue Wege, radioaktiven Abfall zu beseitigen. Ich sehe da kein Problem, warum es nicht so weitergehen kann und ...

Q: Es besteht immer das Risiko von Terroristenangriffen auf ein Atomkraftwerk.

A: Ja, sicher, aber auch wenn Terroristen unser Leben bedrohen, heißt das nicht, dass wir unser Leben deswegen ändern müssen. Wenn wir das tun, haben sie schon gewonnen. Es ist besser, gute Sicherheitsmaßnahmen zu ergreifen, zum Beispiel ...

▸ Look at the card and read the two statements in the speech bubbles.

▸ Choose ONE and think how you can convey and expand on its main ideas.

▸ Begin the discussion by outlining your point of view (this should take no more than one minute).

▸ You must then be prepared to respond to anything the examiner might say and to justify your point of view.

▸ You may be required to explain something you have said, to respond to an opposing point of view expressed by the examiner, or to defend your expressed opinion(s)

▸ You may make notes in your preparation time and refer to them during this part of the examination.

Wie überredet man Jugendliche, keine Verbrechen zu begehen?

Was wichtig ist, ist die Strafe. Jugendlichen muss es klar werden, dass Verbrechen ernsthafte Folgen mit sich bringen. Geldstrafen und Haftstrafen müssen als Abschreckung dienen. Sonst werden sie ihr Benehmen nicht ändern.

Man muss immer deutlich erklären, was die Folgen von Verbrechen sind. Es ist wichtig, dass Jugendliche begreifen, wie ihr Verbrechen das Leben von anderen zerstören kann. Es ist auch wichtig, dass man Jugendlichen andere Alternativen bietet wie sportliche oder kulturelle Möglichkeiten.

Read and listen to a section of this student's oral exam based on Speaking Test B (CD track 2). It is the part where the examiner begins to challenge his views.

E: Die meisten Kriminellen begehen weitere Verbrechen, nachdem sie aus dem Gefängnis kommen. Bedeutet das nicht, dass Gefängnisse sinnlos sind?

S: Nein, dem stimme ich nicht zu. Ohne Furcht vor Haftstrafen wird es viel mehr Verbrechen geben. Da bin ich sicher. Wenn ein Krimineller nach einer Haftstrafe wieder Verbrechen begeht, könnte man sagen, dass der Gefängnisaufenthalt zu bequem und einfach war. Haftstrafen sollten länger und viel unbequemer sein.

E: Wenn ein Krimineller aus einer schwierigen Umwelt kommt, wie kann ihm das Leben im Gefängnis helfen?

S: Man muss ihm zeigen, wie er ein anständiges Leben führen kann, wie er zum Beispiel arbeiten kann, um sich und seine Familie zu ernähren. Man könnte ihm eine Ausbildung anbieten, damit er arbeiten kann, wenn er wieder entlassen wird.

E: Muss man also jeden Kriminellen nach seinem ersten Verbrechen ins Gefängnis schicken?

S: Nein, das habe ich nicht gemeint. Wichtig ist, dass jeder, der gegen das Gesetz verstößt, weiß, dass er sein Verbrechen irgendwie wieder gutmachen muss. Wenn ein Jugendlicher beispielsweise einige Tage damit verbringen müsste, die Straßen zu reinigen, würde er lernen, dass sein Benehmen unangenehme Folgen gehabt hat. Vielleicht würde er dann nachdenken, bevor er wieder ein Verbrechen begeht.

E: Glauben Sie nicht, dass es Fälle gibt, wo es besser wäre, einfach mit den jungen Kriminellen zu sprechen und ihnen zu erklären, dass das, was sie gemacht haben, nicht in Ordnung ist?

S: Im Gegenteil. Ich bin der Meinung, dass solche Kriminellen uns auslachen. Wie werden sie ihr Benehmen ändern, wenn sie keine Strafe bekommen? Man muss ihnen zeigen und nicht nur sagen, dass Verbrechen nicht in Ordnung sind. Sonst machen sie das immer wieder, davon bin ich überzeugt.

Learn some useful phrases for disagreeing (politely!) with the examiner. Examples include:

Nein, im Gegenteil. Ich glaube, dass …

Ich bin überhaupt nicht der gleichen Meinung, weil …

Meiner Meinung nach ist das nicht richtig, weil …

Es stimmt nicht, dass …

Ja, vielleicht, aber man darf nicht vergessen, dass …

The conversation on topics you have studied

Here are some practice questions for each kind of topic:

A region

▶ Für welche Aspekte der Geografie dieser Gegend interessieren Sie sich?
▶ Erzählen Sie mir etwas von der Geschichte dieser Gegend!
▶ Was sind die wichtigste Industrien der Gegend?
▶ Was für soziale oder wirtschaftliche Probleme hat diese Gegend?
▶ Wie sind die Einwohner dieser Gegend?
▶ Wie hat die Gegend sich in letzter Zeit verändert?
▶ Spielt Tourismus eine wichtige Rolle hier?
▶ Würden Sie gern hier leben und arbeiten?

An historical period

▶ Was sind die Hauptereignisse dieses Zeitalters?
▶ Was sind die Ursachen dieser Ereignisse?
▶ Was für Auswirkungen haben sie auf das Zeitalter gehabt?
▶ Haben sie auch heute noch einen Einfluss?
▶ Erzählen Sie mir etwas von einer wichtigen Person aus dieser Zeit!
▶ Wie beurteilen Sie die Ideen dieser Zeit?
▶ Hätten Sie gern in diesem Zeitalter gelebt?

A person (author / poet / dramatist / director / architect / musician / painter)

▶ Beschreiben Sie die kulturellen Einflüsse auf diesen/diese Schriftsteller/in (Dichter/in, Musiker/in usw.).
▶ Was sind seine/ihre Hauptthemen und wie werden diese Themen in seinen/ihren Werken ausgedrückt?
▶ Welches Buch (Theaterstück usw.) bewundern Sie am meisten und warum?
▶ Gibt es Dinge, die Sie in seinen/ihren Werken nicht mögen? Warum?
▶ Wie hat sein/ihr Leben seine/ihre Werke beeinflusst?
▶ Mögen Jugendliche seine/ihre Werke? Warum (nicht)?
▶ Warum mögen Sie persönlich seine/ihre Werke?

Listen to ten students answering sample questions (CD track 3). You'll find the transcripts in a word document on the CD ROM.

The Listening, Reading and Writing paper

You can plan your time as you wish, but it is suggested that you allocate your time roughly as follows:

> half an hour for the listening questions in Section A
>
> one hour for the reading and writing questions in Section A
>
> one hour for the essay question in Section B.

Section A: Listening, Reading and Writing (70 marks)

Listening

There will be about five minutes of recording altogether and you will be able to play it, replay it and pause it yourself. There will be four passages with various types of question in German, for example:

‣ missing numbers which you have to complete

‣ true, false or not in text phrases

‣ ticking those statements which are true

‣ sentences with words or phrases missing and three possible answers.

Reading and Writing

First, there will be three different types of questions in German, such as:

‣ choosing words from a box to complete gaps in the text

‣ reading a number of texts, then matching summary sentences to them

‣ reading a text and marking statements about it *'richtig'*, *'falsch'* or *'nicht angegeben'*.

Then there will be two translation questions:

‣ translating a short passage of German into English

‣ translating English sentences into German.

Section B: Writing an Essay on a Cultural Topic

You have to write one essay of **at least** 250 words on **one** of the two cultural topics you have studied. There will be a choice of two essay questions on each topic. So if you have studied, say, an author and a period of history, you will have four questions to choose from, two on each topic.

The key ways to prepare are by:

‣ doing plenty of listening practice to keep your ear 'tuned in' to German

‣ reading a wide variety of materials linked to the topics listed on page 4

‣ practising writing 250-word essays on cultural topics in about an hour

‣ working through the exam-type questions and tips on the following pages (the answers are on page 49).

Schlechte Chancen für Ausländer CD track 4

Sie hören jetzt einen Bericht über die Ausbildungs- und Arbeitsmöglichkeiten von Ausländern in Deutschland. Lesen Sie die Aussagen unten. In jeder Aussage fehlt eine Zahl. Schreiben Sie die richtigen Zahlen in die Textlücken.

i) Es gibt in der Bundesrepublik ungefähr _____ Millionen Ausländer.

ii) 2007 verliessen _____ Prozent der Ausländerkinder die Schule ohne Abschluss.

iii) Im Jahr 2003 betrug diese Zahl _____ Prozent.

iv) _____ Prozent der ausländischen Jugendlichen haben keine Berufsausbildung.

v) Unter den in Deutschland lebenden Türken haben _____ Prozent keine Berufsqualifikationen.

vi) Bei den Italienern beträgt diese Zahl _____ Prozent.

> You will hear quite a lot of figures and this can be quite confusing. When you first listen, note down all the figures you hear. On your second listening, make notes of all the words before and after each figure, then compare them to the sentences above. This should help you work out which figure goes where.

Die 15 Millionen Zuwanderer in Deutschland bekommen nur mit Mühe einen Job, einen vernünftigen Schulabschluss oder eine Berufsausbildung. Das zeigt der neue Integrationsbericht der Bundesregierung. Jedes sechste Zuwandererkind verlässt die Schule immer noch ohne Abschluss. Die Integrationsbeauftragte der Bundesregierung, Maria Böhmer (CDU), berichtete, dass die Zuwanderer dramatisch schlechte Chancen in der Schule und auf dem Arbeitsmarkt haben. Nach ihrem Bericht verliessen im Jahr 2007 17,5 Prozent der Ausländerkinder die Schule ohne Abschluss. Diese Zahl ist etwas niedriger als 2003, als es noch 19,2 Prozent waren, aber noch immer in keinster Weise befriedigend. Und die meisten derjenigen, die einen Abschluss machen, besuchen die Hauptschule.

Als echtes Alarmzeichen bewertete Böhmer die Lage auf dem Ausbildungsmarkt. Laut dieses Berichts haben 40 Prozent der Jugendlichen aus Ausländerfamilien keinerlei Berufsausbildung.

Überdurchschnittlich betroffen sind davon Zuwanderer aus der Türkei, Italien und Griechenland. So haben 72 Prozent aller in Deutschland lebenden Türken oder Türkischstämmigen keine berufliche Qualifizierung. Bei den Griechen sind es 61 Prozent, bei den Italienern 56. Diese Entwicklung setze sich auch bei der zweiten und dritten Generation fort, die vielfach in Deutschland geboren wurde, sagte Böhmer.

Entsprechend gering sind die Chancen der Zuwanderer auf dem Arbeitsmarkt: Ihr Risiko, arbeitslos zu werden, ist doppelt so hoch wie bei den Deutschen. Dieser Teufelskreis aus geringer Bildung, fehlender Ausbildung und hoher Arbeitslosigkeit müsse überwunden werden, forderte Böhmer. „Wir können auf kein Talent verzichten."

Gar nicht so öko   CD track 5

Sie hören jetzt einen Bericht über Öl und Heizung. Lesen Sie die Aussagen unten. Schreiben Sie den richtigen Buchstaben ins Kästchen, so dass die Aussagen mit dem Sinn des Berichts übereinstimmen.

a) Die Regierung will ☐ als erneuerbare Energie fördern.

  A Luft
  B Öl
  C Wärmepumpe

b) Das Gerät wandelt ☐ aus der Erde um.

  A Wind
  B Energie
  C Luft

c) Man meint, es sei ☐.

  A unsicher
  B umweltfeindlich
  C ökologisch

d) Die Kunden sind vom ☐ unabhängig.

  A Ölpreis
  B Strompreis
  C Energiebedarf

e) Die Pumpen benutzen ☐.

  A Wasser
  B Öl
  C Elektrizität

f) Die Ökobilanz kann in einigen Fällen ☐ sein.

  A positiv
  B genauso hoch
  C negativ

> Read the sentences and possible solutions carefully. Listen carefully as this is designed to test your understanding of the report. Make notes. Sometimes you may hear more than one of the words in the report. It is the context that you are being tested on, e.g in the last question both **Strompreis** and **Ölpreis** are mentioned in the same sentence but listen carefully to decide which is being described in connection with **abhängig** and which one with **unabhängig**.

Was tun, wenn der steigende Ölpreis bald auch die Heizkosten sprengt? Die Bundesregierung will die Wärmepumpe als erneuerbare Energie fördern. Doch die Ökobilanz der Erdwärme-Heizung ist umstritten.

Als zukunftssichere Alternative zu jetzigen Heizsystemen preist das süddeutsche Energieunternehmen seinen Kunden die Wärmepumpe an. Das Gerät wandelt Energie aus der Erde um. Damit lässt sich beispielsweise eine Fußbodenheizung betreiben. Die Wärmepumpe gilt als ökologisch, weil sie einen großen Anteil der Energie umweltfreundlich aus dem Boden oder der Luft holt, ohne dass das Treibhausgas Kohlendioxid anfällt. Dank ihrer eigenen Wärmepumpe sind die Kunden unabhängig vom Ölpreis.

Das Marketing ist erfolgreich. Schon jetzt sind nach Angaben des Bundesverbands 300 000 solche Geräte in deutschen Haushalten installiert – ein neuer Rekord. Im vergangenen Jahr wurden mehr als 45 000 Stück verkauft. Das ist mehr als im Jahr 2006, obwohl der Wärmemarkt insgesamt stagnierte.

Vom Ölpreis sind die Kunden vielleicht unabhängig, aber noch nicht vom Strompreis, denn eine Wärmepumpe verbraucht auch elektrische Energie. Allerdings bieten zur Zeit alle vier großen Stromkonzerne günstige Tarife für Wärmepumpen an.

Es gibt jedoch ein Problem: Jede Wärmepumpe kostet etwa 15 000 Euro und verbraucht Strom, der in Deutschland zurzeit vor allem aus klimaschädigendem Kohlestrom kommt, insbesondere im Winter, wenn viel geheizt wird. In manchen Fällen kann die Ökobilanz daher sogar negativ sein.

Die Schnellzug-Ära beginnt erst
CD track 6

Sie hören jetzt einen Bericht über Schnellzüge. Lesen Sie die Aussagen unten. Schreiben Sie jeweils R (richtig), F (falsch) oder NA (nicht angegeben) neben die Aussagen.

a)	Es wird eine Schnellzugstrecke zwischen München Hauptbahnhof und Flughafen geben.	
b)	Es bedeutet nicht das Ende der Superschnellzüge in Europa.	
c)	Bis 2025 wird es in Europa mehr als 30 000 km neue Hochgeschwindigskeitsstrecken geben.	
d)	Der ICE wird von Siemens hergestellt.	
e)	Der Velaro E fährt mit 350 km/Stunde durch Spanien.	
f)	In Deutschland wird eine neue Strecke von Berlin nach Hamburg geplant.	
g)	Wenn sich die Geschwindigkeit verdoppelt, verdoppelt sich auch der Luftwiderstand.	
h)	Man braucht besondere aerodynamische Lösungen, damit ein Schnellzug auf den Schienen bleibt.	
i)	Komfort ist nicht so wichtig wie Geschwindigkeit und Wirtschaftlichkeit.	

> You need to understand small details to work out whether the statements say the same thing as the listening text. Listen carefully and make notes. Be aware that there will only be one or two pieces of information that could be classified as **NA** (*nicht angegeben*). In order for this classification to be valid, there should be no mention of the fact at all in the text. It is very easy to confuse **NA** and **F** (*falsch*). For a statement to be classified as false, the information must be given **incorrectly**.

Der politische Kampf um den Hochgeschwindigkeitszug Transrapid währte lange, doch im März kam das Aus: Die Strecke zwischen dem Münchner Hauptbahnhof und dem Flughafen vor den Toren der Stadt wird nicht gebaut. Doch das Scheitern dieses Projekts bedeutet nicht das Ende der Superschnellzug-Ära. Diese steht Deutschland, Frankreich, Spanien, Italien und Russland erst noch bevor. In diesen Ländern entstehen bis 2025 mehr als 10 000 Kilometer neue Hochgeschwindigkeitsstrecken, berichtet das Wissenschaftsmagazin *Bild der Wissenschaft*.

In Zügen wie dem französischen TGV und dem ICE des deutschen Herstellers Siemens und dessen Weiterentwicklungen sind hohe Geschwindigkeiten bereits Alltag: Der TGV wie auch der ICE 3 erreicht auf einigen Strecken bereits planmäßig Geschwindigkeiten von 320 Kilometern pro Stunde. Ab 2009 soll der Velaro E, das jüngste Serienprodukt aus der Siemens-Familie, mit 350 Kilometern pro Stunde zwischen Madrid und Barcelona verkehren.

Eines der Kernprobleme bei der Entwicklung von Hochgeschwindigkeitszügen: Verdoppelt sich die Geschwindigkeit, so vervierfacht sich der Luftwiderstand und die für den Antrieb benötigte Leistung steigt um den Faktor acht. An diesen physikalischen Grundsätzen kann auch die beste Ingenieurskunst nichts ändern. Damit ein vergleichsweise leichter Zug auch bei Tempo 400 auf den Schienen bleiben kann, ohne abzuheben, sind besondere aerodynamische Lösungen erforderlich. Eine längere Schnauze und Flügelstummel könnten den Zügen ausreichende Bodenhaftung verschaffen. Bis der erste doppelstöckige NGT durch Europa sausen wird, ist freilich noch viel Entwicklungsarbeit nötig. Denn verbessert werden sollen nicht nur Geschwindigkeit und Wirtschaftlichkeit, sondern auch der Komfort für die Reisenden.

Interview mit Julia Jentsch   CD track 7

Sie hören jetzt ein Interview mit Julia Jentsch. Lesen Sie die Aussagen unten und kreuzen Sie die sechs Sätze an, die falsch sind.

a)	Julia Jentsch hat vor drei Jahren die Rolle von Sophie Scholl gespielt.	
b)	Sophie Scholl war Nationalsozialistin.	
c)	Liza ist Nazianhängerin.	
d)	Liza kann die Ideologie nicht kritisch sehen.	
e)	Sie will keine Kinder haben.	
f)	Dieser Film ist eine Tragödie.	
g)	Jiri Menzel ist der bekannteste Filmemachers Tschechiens.	
h)	Milos Forman ist der Regisseur.	
i)	1970 hat Menzel einen Oscar gewonnen.	
j)	Der neue Film heißt ‚Ich habe den französischen König bedient'.	
k)	Der Film wurde 2006 gedreht.	

• •

This is a simple true-or-false exercise, but you must be careful to read the rubric. In this case, you need to find the six statements which are **false**. Read the statements carefully and then listen carefully to the recording. Try to work out which statements are true as well as those which are false.

• •

Interviewer: Frau Jentsch, vor drei Jahren haben Sie als Widerstandskämpferin Sophie Scholl gegen die Nazis gekämpft. In ‚Ich habe den englischen König bedient' spielen Sie jetzt die sudetendeutsche Nationalsozialistin Liza. Wollten Sie kein Vorbild mehr sein?

Jentsch: Darum ging es nicht – aber ich habe damit gerechnet. Liza fehlt im Gegensatz zu Sophie Scholl der klare Blick für die Diktatur. Sie begeistert sich schnell für eine Ideologie und ist nicht fähig, sie kritisch zu sehen. Sie ist stellvertretend für eine Menge Menschen, die den Nazis damals blind gefolgt sind.

Interviewer: Hatten Sie als good girl des deutschen Kinos keine Bedenken, diese Rolle zu spielen?

Jentsch: Wenn im Vordergrund gestanden hätte, dass Liza eine Nazi-Anhängerin ist, hätte ich keine Lust auf die Rolle gehabt. Es war nicht so, dass ich mir gedacht habe: Oh ja, ich will jetzt unbedingt einmal eine Nazi-Deutsche spielen. Im Gegenteil: Eigentlich kann ich gut darauf verzichten.

Interviewer: In einer Szene starrt Liza auf ein Bild von Hitler, das an der Wand hängt. Sie will dem Reich einen Sohn schenken ...

Jentsch: Als ich die Szene zum ersten Mal im Kino gesehen habe, musste ich zuerst lachen, und dann ist mir fast schlecht geworden. Aber dann wurde mir klar, dass viele deutsche Frauen so wie Liza dem Führer einen Sohn schenken wollten. Das Lachen und die Grausamkeit liegen in diesem Film nah beieinander – so wie im richtigen Leben.

Interviewer: Neben Milos Forman gilt Regisseur Jiri Menzel als berühmtester Filmemacher Tschechiens. Kannten Sie seine Filme, bevor er Ihnen das Drehbuch geschickt hat?

Jentsch: Liebe nach Fahrplan habe ich gesehen. Für den hat er 1968 den Oscar für den besten ausländischen Film bekommen.

Interviewer: Wie ist Menzel auf Sie aufmerksam geworden?

Jentsch: Er hatte seinen Produzenten nach einer deutschen Schauspielerin für die Rolle der Liza gefragt, und irgendwie sind sie auf mich gekommen. Ich bin dann nach Prag geflogen und habe mich mit Menzel in einem kleinen Restaurant getroffen.

Interviewer: ‚Ich habe den englischen König bedient' wurde bereits vor zwei Jahren gedreht. Haben Sie den Film in der Zwischenzeit schon mal gesehen?

Jentsch: Schon ein paarmal sogar. Viele Schauspieler gehen ja während der Premiere aus dem Kino, weil sie den Film schon kennen. Bei diesem Film bin ich aber im Saal geblieben.

Interviewer: ‚Ich habe den englischen König bedient' mit Julia Jentsch läuft am 21. August 2008 in den deutschen Kinos an.

Wir, die Schläger

Lesen Sie den Text unten und beantworten Sie die folgenden Fragen a) und b).

Peter ist jetzt 30, ein sehr höflicher, zurückhaltender Typ mit festem Händedruck und freundlichem Blick. Er arbeitet als Fußballtrainer bei einem deutschen Bundesliga-Club, hat einen Dienstwagen und will demnächst heiraten. Peter hat Glück gehabt, das weiß er. Glück, ein
5 Leben voller Gewalt hinter sich zu haben.

Mit 13 brach Peter in einen Baumarkt ein, mit 14 knackte er Autos und fuhr damit zur Schule, mit 17 lieferte er den Dönerbuden Neuköllns Schnaps, den er zuvor taschenweise geklaut hatte. Tausende von Mark
9 ergaunerte sich der Teenager so, Monat für Monat.

Und während sein Zwillingsbruder, der heute katholischer Priester ist, auf ein glänzendes Abitur zusteuerte, trieb Peter sich auf den Straßen Neuköllns herum und fand, als einer der wenigen Deutschen, dort Anerkennung und Freunde. Zum Beispiel Marek, das Schlitzohr, den Boxer und ‚Meisterdieb‘, wie Peter heute noch sagt. Zusammen überfielen sie Supermärkte, sprayten, klauten, prügelten auch, wenn es sein musste. ‚Es gab jeden Tag was auf die Fresse. So ist das hier im Viertel, entweder
17 du schlägst oder du wirst geschlagen‘, behauptet Marek.

‚Wir konnten nehmen, was wir wollten, und keiner hat uns aufgehalten. Wir fühlten uns unantastbar‘, sagt der 30-Jährige, der inzwischen zwei kleine Kinder hat und bei der Bahn arbeitet. Sie waren noch keine 18, als sie Klamotten von Armani und Versace trugen und mit 18 dann fuhren sie einen Ferrari und Porsche. ‚Heute habe ich manchmal am Ende des Monats keine 20 Euro mehr in der Tasche, aber trotzdem will ich auf keinen Fall zurück in mein altes Leben‘, sagt Marek. ‚Es wäre nicht mehr
25 lange gutgegangen‘.

Mit 21 kaufte er sich einen BMW M 5, ‚320 PS hatte der‘, und raste schnurstracks in sein Verderben: Totalschaden, ein Monat Koma, ein Jahr Rollstuhl und Narben am ganzen Körper. ‚Da bin ich aufgewacht und habe mir gesagt: Jetzt muss sich etwas ändern, sonst gehst du drauf‘.
30 Marek stieg aus.

Auch in Peters Leben gab es diesen Moment, und kein Sozialarbeiter, kein Richter, kein Polizist hat ihn herbeigeführt. Er hat es alleine geschafft, und darauf ist er stolz. Seinen Traum, Fußballprofi zu werden, hatte er wegen einer Knieverletzung aufgeben müssen, doch ein großer Berliner Verein stellte den damals 21-Jährigen als Jugendtrainer ein. Plötzlich spürte Peter Verantwortung, Anerkennung, Erfolg. ‚Ich habe mich in meinen Spielern wiedererkannt und mir sagen müssen: Genau so ein
38 aggressiver Trottel warst du auch‘.

The Listening, Reading and Writing paper

a) (lines 1–17) Lesen Sie die Aussagen unten und kreuzen Sie die sechs Sätze an, die falsch sind.

i)	Peter hat jetzt einen festen Beruf.	
ii)	Peter verdiente nichts.	
iii)	Mit 14 hatte Peter sein eigenes Auto.	
iv)	Peter hat eine Schwester.	
v)	Peter war zwei Jahre in Gefängnis.	
vi)	Es gab fast keine anderen Deutschen auf den Straßen von Neukölln.	
vii)	Peter kannte keine Grenzen.	
viii)	Peter lieferte Zigaretten.	
ix)	Marek war Pazifist.	

b) (lines 18–38) Beantworten Sie die folgenden Fragen auf Deutsch. Geben Sie nur kurze Antworten.

i) Was macht Marek jetzt von Beruf?

ii) Was ist Marek passiert, dass er sein Leben so umwandelte?

iii) Wie hat Peter es geschafft, sein Leben zu ändern?

iv) Was war Peters Traumjob?

v) Was macht Peter jetzt von Beruf?

Read the text carefully and make sure you are referring to the correct part and to the correct person in your answer. It can be easy to get mixed up with (b) questions i), iv) and v) as they all refer to jobs. Be careful to base your answers on what it says in the text and not on things you know or believe to be true.

15-Jährige wegen Misshandlung verurteilt

Lesen Sie den Bericht über eine Gewalttat und die Aussagen unten. Schreiben Sie jeweils R (richtig), F (falsch) oder NA (nicht angegeben) neben die Aussagen.

Sie quälten andere Mädchen mit brennenden Zigaretten und glühenden Drähten – und filmten ihre Taten mit dem Handy: Wegen stundenlanger Misshandlung wurden zwei 15-jährige Mädchen zu Jugendarrest und Sozialstunden verurteilt.

Frankfurt am Main – Das Gericht in Frankfurt am Main sah es als erwiesen an, dass das Schlägerduo Mitte Mai die anderen beiden Schülerinnen in einer Gartenlaube mit brennenden Zigaretten, einem Besenstiel, glühenden Drähten und einem Teppichmesser traktierten und ihre Taten mit dem Handy filmten. Hintergrund ist offenbar ein Konflikt zwischen zwei rivalisierenden Frankfurter Mädchen-Gangs.

Die beiden 15-Jährigen hatten ihre späteren Opfer offenbar rein zufällig auf einem S-Bahnhof getroffen und sie wegen kürzlicher Streitigkeiten zur Rede stellen wollen. Dabei soll einer Freundin der beiden Verurteilten von Freunden der Opfer die Nase gebrochen worden sein.

Als sich die 14- und die 13-Jährigen nicht so verhielten, wie es die 15-Jährigen wollten, zwangen sie die Jüngeren, mit ihnen in eine Kleingartensiedlung zu kommen. Auf dem Weg dorthin schlugen sie weiterhin auf die Mädchen ein, bis die Ältere mehrere blutende Wunden hatte.

Anschließend zwangen die beiden ihre Opfer, mit ihnen in einen Garten einzusteigen. Dort fesselten sie die 13-Jährige mit Draht an einen Gartenstuhl, nachdem sie sich bis auf die Unterhose hatte ausziehen müssen.

Danach schlugen beide das Mädchen mit Fäusten und einem Besenstiel, drückten Zigaretten auf ihrer Haut aus und zwangen die 14-Jährige, ihre jüngere Freundin mit Erde zu füttern. Der Richter bezeichnete das Vorgehen der Angreiferinnen als ‚mies, erbärmlich und widerlich'.

a)	Die Gewalttäterinnen sind 15 Jahre alt.	
b)	Die Opfer sind auch 15 Jahre alt.	
c)	Die Täter und Opfer kannten sich nicht.	
d)	Die Gewalttat passierte in Frankfurt.	
e)	Die Gewalttat wurde mit einem Handy aufgenommen.	
f)	Die Gewalttat ist in der S-Bahn passiert.	
g)	Das jüngste Mädchen wurde am schlimmsten behandelt.	
h)	Der Richter war schockiert.	
i)	Die Mädchen wurde nur zu Jugendarrest verurteilt.	

> You must take care with this type of exercise and read both the text and the statements carefully as they will not be exactly the same. Again, take care with **NA** as there will rarely be more than one or two in a text like this.

The Listening, Reading and Writing paper

Übersetzen Sie ins Englische:

In vielen Ländern der Erde fehlen Medikamente, und es sterben jedes Jahr etwa 2,2 Millionen Menschen an Durchfall. Jeder zweite Tote in den Entwicklungsländern erliegt einer Infektionen – das sind rund sechs Millionen Menschen jährlich. Zu 90 Prozent sind diese Krankheiten unbedeutend. Nur, wenn man keine Medikamente hat, können sie tödlich sein – so entsteht aus einer leichten Bronchitis schnell eine Lungenentzündung.

Vereinfacht kann man sagen, dass die Hälfte der Weltbevölkerung – drei Milliarden Menschen – keinen Zugang zu Arzneimitteln hat. Doch häufig ist nicht der zu hohe Preis für Medikamente Schuld, sondern die mangelnde Verfügbarkeit vor Ort. Selbst wenn westliche Pharmahersteller ihre Medikamente verschenken, erreichen sie oft nicht die betroffene Bevölkerung.

> Beware of 'false friends' or words which look like an English word, but mean something different. Think carefully about the translation of words such as 'Medikamente'.

> Remember that a literal translation will not always sound right in English. What expression would be better than 'developing countries' for 'Entwicklungsländer'? What word will you use to translate 'erliegt'?

> Where possible, keep your English translation closely in line with the German because doing so cuts down the risk of missing out parts of the sentence. But sometimes the English version will sound more natural if you alter the word order a little. Remember that German word order is very different from English and this can affect meaning. Do not forget the verb at the end of the sentence.

Übersetzen Sie ins Deutsche:

a Without medicine, many simple illnesses are fatal.
b It is often very difficult to reach the people affected.
c Many people in the Third World die every year from diarrhoea.
d The price of medicine is often very high.
e Medicine is often sent as a gift by the pharmaceutical companies.

> Think grammatically! What does each sentence require you to do? Remember that German word order is different from English. You need to take that into account when translating.

> Remember that you can't always translate word for word. The best translation for 'sent as a gift' is only a single word in German.

Writing an Essay on a Cultural Topic

You have to write one essay of at least 250 words on one of the cultural topics you have studied. The three vital stages are planning, writing and checking.

Planning

Don't rush this stage. 5–10 minutes thinking about the question, deciding on your argument and dividing it into paragraphs, jotting down the facts you want to use and thinking out a good introduction and conclusion is time well spent. Keep referring to the title to make sure every paragraph is relevant to the question. You might also note vocabulary and phrases you want to use in each paragraph. Then, when everything is in order, start writing, and make sure you stick to the plan.

Writing

Work through your notes for each paragraph. Write them up using a variety of sentence lengths, interesting vocabulary and a range of grammatical constructions. Be especially careful about the links between the paragraphs, so the examiner can follow the argument easily. A phrase like ‚Man muss zugeben, dass ...‘ can introduce ideas which build on those in the previous paragraph, but if you want to move on to a different angle you might start with ‚Wenn man überlegt ...‘ or ‚Aber man muss auch sagen, dass ...‘

Checking

Read through your essay once to check the flow of ideas and make sure each sentence makes sense. Then do a more detailed check, looking especially for these common errors:

▶ verbs which don't agree with their subject or are in the wrong tense
▶ adjectives which don't match the noun they describe
▶ phrases which are not idiomatic and don't sound German
▶ misspellings, especially of words similar to, but not the same as, English
▶ missing umlauts
▶ word order: time – manner – place phrases, verbs in the correct place, past participles at the end of the sentence.

The marks for this question are awarded as follows:

▶ **content**: 25 marks, i.e. a through understanding of the topic, with relevant examples and well-justified opinions and a well-structured, logical argument
▶ **vocabulary**: 5 marks, i.e. a wide range of words specific to the topic and also good 'essay phrases'
▶ **use of complex structures**: 5 marks, i.e. including a range of tenses, the subjunctive, conjunctions, relative clauses with correct word order
▶ **accuracy**: 5 marks, i.e. including all correct verb endings and tenses, adjective endings, correct genders and correct word order.

All the grammar you learned for AS is still needed, and there are some extra points for A2. **Pages 25–31 revise AS grammar, reminding you what you should know and giving you phrases and sentences to translate from and into German for practice. Pages 32–33 revise the points you will be learning on the A2 course, also practised through sentences to translate.**

Grammar is even more important at A2 than it was at AS. So, what can you to do make sure you really do know your stuff?

Pay attention when grammar is explained. If you learn the rules and the exceptions and do some practice exercises, you will be surprised how much of it will stick.

Accept that there is quite a lot of detail to master and be prepared to go over things regularly. Re-read your grammar notes, re-do practice exercises, ask questions if you come across things you don't fully understand.

Be pro-active. Go through marked written work, looking carefully at the things which have been corrected. Decide which ones are 'silly mistakes', caused by forgetting things which you know well and make a list of them, so you can try to avoid them in future. Then look for errors where you are not quite sure why it is wrong. Ask, if necessary, then look up that grammar point in the grammar section of your textbook and in the relevant section of the grammar workbook. Keep practising and asking questions until you do understand it. When you understand it, review it by writing grammar notes on it in your own words, adding examples.

Make a list of example sentences from your written work which use some of the more complex grammar points well. Learn them, and use them as models for other sentences with different vocabulary but which use the same basic structure. Make a point of including a good variety of grammatical structures in the practice essays you write.

Work through the exercises on the following pages. If there are practice sentences you find hard to translate, learn the correct version from the answer section by heart.

Revision of AS Grammar: nouns, adjectives, adverbs

Check the grammar section of *Zeitgeist 2* and/or the Grammar Workbook if you need to know more about any of these things:

▶ typical masculine endings for nouns, such as *-ant, -er, -ich, -ig, -ing, -ismus,* etc

▶ typical feminine endings for nouns, such as *-e, -heit, -ik, -in, keit, -schaft, -ung,* etc

▶ typical neuter endings for nouns, such as *-chen, -lein, -um,* etc

▶ how to form the plurals of nouns – is it *-n, -en, -nen, -s, -er* and does it have an umlaut? Or does it require a plural at all?

▶ how to make adjectives agree in number and case

▶ forming possessive adjectives like *mein, dein, sein, ihr, unser,* etc

▶ using *kein* with appropriate endings to translate the negative

▶ using adjectives as adverbs

▶ comparing adjectives by adding *-er* plus the appropriate adjective ending

▶ using the superlative by adding *-(e)st* to the adjective as well as the appropriate ending and not forgetting the definite article *der, die* or *das*

▶ using irregular comparisons like *besser* and *höher* or irregular superlatives like *(das) beste* and *(das) nächste.*

(1) Translate into English:

1 Man muss kälteres Wasser in der Waschmaschine benutzen.
2 Die Ausbeutung der Wälder zeigt keinen Respekt für die Natur.
3 Das nächste Mal erwarten wir etwas Besseres!
4 Kohlendioxid hat die schlimmste Auswirkung auf unserer Atmosphäre.
5 Wir haben keine realistischeren Lösungen.
6 Was muss man machen, um den richtigen Weg zu finden?
7 Die Transportsysteme der Zukunft werden viel effizienter sein.
8 Eine reichhaltige Diät ist besser für die Gesundheit.
9 Klar bin ich viel optimistischer als du!
10 Die Sonne ist eine direkte Quelle von Licht und Wärme.

Translate into German:

11 Trains are more environmentally friendly than cars.
12 We have enough gas, but no petrol.
13 An old car is not good for the environment.
14 A new car is just as bad as an old one.
15 Their house has solar panels.
16 My central heating is expensive.
17 There's a good atmosphere in the eco-village.
18 People there live more cheaply than we do.
19 Do you recycle old newspapers and empty bottles?
20 Which energy is the cheapest?

Revision of AS Grammar: pronouns

Check the grammar section of *Zeitgeist 2* and/or the Grammar Workbook if you need to know more about any of these things:

- ▶ direct object pronouns: *mich, dich, sich, uns, euch, ihnen*
- ▶ indirect object pronouns: *mir, dir, sich*
- ▶ reflexive pronouns used with reflexive verbs: *mich, dich, sich, uns, euch*
- ▶ the relative pronouns *der, die, das, dessen, deren*
- ▶ indefinite pronouns *jemand, niemand, jeder.*

(2) Translate into English:

1 Immigranten? Bezahlt man ihnen Kindergeld?
2 Laut des deutschen Grundgesetzes darf niemand wegen seiner Rasse benachteiligt werden.
3 Immigranten sind mit ihren Familien nach Deutschland gekommen.
4 In den letzten hundert Jahren haben deutsche Aussiedler wegen ihrer Nationalität viel gelitten.
5 Jeder hat das Recht auf die Nationalität vom Land seiner Geburt.
6 Immigranten sind zum Arbeiten in unser Land gekommen.
7 Wir sind gegen jeden, der die Menschenrechte nicht respektiert.
8 Deutschland ist das Land, in dem ich aufgewachsen bin und dessen Kultur ich mich anzupassen versuche.
9 Man erlaubt mir nicht, meine Herkunft zu vergessen.
10 Man wird nirgendwo als zugehörig betrachtet.

Translate into German:

11 Explain racism to me.
12 I told them I do not understand them.
13 He lives in Leipzig now and finds it very peaceful.
14 It is a town that I don't know.
15 Guest workers are mainly Turks, who came to Germany for work.
16 The resettlers are Germans who now live in Eastern Europe.
17 They have lived there for 20 years.
18 The map? Show me it, please.
19 Xenophobia – what is the cause?
20 We must try to replace it with tolerance.

Revision of AS Grammar: infinitives and the present tense

Check the grammar section of *Zeitgeist 2* and/or the Grammar Workbook if you need to know more about any of these things:

▶ the use of the infinitive construction with *zu*
▶ the use of modal verbs plus the infinitive
▶ the infinitive with *um ... zu*
▶ the present tense of regular verbs such as *wohnen, leben, arbeiten*
▶ the present tense of the modal verbs *wollen, sollen, dürfen, mögen*
▶ the present tense of irregular verbs such as *gehen, fahren, haben, sein, werden*
▶ the use of the present tense with *seit*
▶ the use of some verbs which take the dative such as *helfen, geben*.

(3) Translate into English:

1 Wie sind diese Probleme zu lösen?
2 Machen Sie schon etwas, um Geld für eine Wohlfahrtsorganisation aufzubringen?
3 Was brauchen solche Wohlfahrtsorganisationen, um funktionieren zu können?
4 Wir müssen eine langfristige Lösung finden.
5 Ohne Job kann man die Miete nicht bezahlen.
6 Ohne Unterkunft ist es schwierig, einen Job zu finden.
7 Wir versuchen, diesen Leuten zu helfen, ihre Gesellschaft wieder aufzubauen.
8 Den Entwicklungsländern sollte erlaubt sein, ihre Schulden bei den Industrieländern zu vergessen.
9 Wir dürfen nicht vergessen, dass alle Menschen Hilfe brauchen.
10 Wenn man in absoluter Armut lebt, hat man nicht genug zu essen.

Translate into German:

11 Everyone should have a certain standard of living.
12 Do you work for a charity?
13 I want to help people to have a future.
14 In many countries, lots of people cannot write or read.
15 I hope to be able to help them.
16 She wants to go to Africa to help the children there.
17 We have been working there for ten years.
18 Life can be very difficult for single mothers.
19 Lots of young people want to be rich.
20 What do you do if you can't find a job?

Revision of AS Grammar: past tenses

Check the grammar section of *Zeitgeist 2* and/or the Grammar Workbook if you need to know more about any of these things:

> ▶ the perfect tense with *haben*: *ich habe ... gemacht, ich habe ... gespielt*
> ▶ the perfect tense with *sein*: *ich bin ... gegangen, ich bin ... gefahren*
> ▶ the perfect tense of irregular verbs: *ich habe gesehen, ich habe gegessen*
> ▶ the perfect tense of separable verbs: *ich bin ... abgefahren, ich habe ... festgestellt*
> ▶ the imperfect tense: *er stand, ich sah, wir gingen*
> ▶ the pluperfect tense: *er hatte ... gesehen, ich war ... gegangen*
> ▶ the perfect tense of the passive voice: *es wurde verkauft.*

(4) Translate into English:

1 Der Dichter Johann Wolfgang von Goethe wurde 1749 geboren.
2 Karl Wilhelm Gropius hat eine Ausbildung als Landschaftsmaler in Berlin gemacht.
3 In dieser Zeit wurde die Gesellschaft von Männern beherrscht.
4 Fassbinder wurde 1945 geboren und verbrachte seine Kindheit in einem chaotischen Nachkriegsdeutschland.
5 Marlene Dietrich ist in Berlin und Dessau zur Schule gegangen.
6 Im April 1930 hat sie Deutschland verlassen und ist nach Amerika ausgewandert.
7 Roland Emmerich begann seine Karriere als Regisseur in Deutschland.
8 Später hat er Ruhm in Amerika gefunden.
9 Der erste erfolgreiche Film von Wim Wenders war ‚Paris, Texas‘ (1984).
10 Sein Film ‚Der Himmel über Berlin‘ (1987) hat den Film ‚Stadt der Engel‘ (1998) mit Meg Ryan und Nicholas Cage inspiriert.

Translate into German:

11 How many people visited the Pergamon Museum in 2007?
12 This painting was sold for $78,000,000 last year.
13 Christa Wolf was born in 1929.
14 She did not believe in the dismantling of the GDR state.
15 At first, Lessing studied medicine and theology in Leipizig.
16 Later, he lived as a writer in Berlin, where he wrote for several newspapers.
17 In 1995, Franka Potente won the Bavarian Film Prize for Young Talent.
18 Tom Tykwer wrote the role of Lola in the film "Run, Lola, Run" for her.
19 Franka Potente has also written a screenplay.
20 Annette von Droste-Hülshoff wrote beautiful ballads and poems about Westphalia.

Revision of AS Grammar: future and conditional

Check the grammar section of *Zeitgeist 2* and/or the Grammar Workbook if you need to know more about any of these things:

▶ using the present tense to refer to things which are going to happen soon, with mention of a future time: *Morgen gehe ich ins Kino, nächste Woche bleiben wir hier.*
▶ using *werden* + infinitive to refer to precise future plans: *ich werde ... wohnen, wir werden ... sehen*
▶ using *ich möchte* + infinitive to describe something that you would like to happen: *ich möchte ... arbeiten*
▶ forming the conditional tense using imperfect subjunctive of *werden* + infinitive to say what would happen in certain circumstances: *wir würden ... verbringen*
▶ using *wenn* with the conditional/imperfect subjunctive. (NB: unlike English, the same tense must be used in both parts of the sentence)
▶ forming the imperfect subjunctive: *ich wäre, ich hätte, ich ginge, ich käme.*

(5) Translate into English:

1 Morgen werden wir in einer Welt voller Computer leben.
2 In der Zukunft werden Computer Ihnen helfen, alles zu erledigen.
3 Es wird nicht mehr nötig sein, aus dem Hause zu gehen, weil man zu Hause alles haben wird, was man braucht.
4 Die Entscheidungen der Wissenschaftler werden ernste Folgen haben.
5 Aufgrund der Gentechnik wird es möglich sein, viele Erbkrankheiten zu heilen.
6 Aber in den nächsten fünf Jahren wird es keine Wunderheilmittel geben.
7 Das Manipulieren von menschlichem Erbgut könnte eine Welt voller perfekter Menschen schaffen.
8 Alle Lebensmittel werden gentechnisch verändert werden.
9 Gentechnisch veränderte Lebensmittel könnten neue Allergien verursachen.
10 Wenn man wüsste, dass solche Lebensmittel unschädlich wären, könnte man damit die Ernährungsprobleme in den Entwicklungsländern lösen.

Translate into German:

11 How will we live in the future?
12 There will be computers everywhere.
13 We will do our shopping on the Internet.
14 You'll be able to spend your holiday on the moon.
15 What will daily life be like?
16 My computer will help me make decisions.
17 Scientists will have to be very responsible.
18 I would not like to live in a perfect world.
19 People should know more about technology.
20 If I were young, I would study I.T.

Grammar

Revision of AS Grammar: negatives

Check the grammar section of *Zeitgeist 2* and/or the Grammar Workbook if you need to know more about any of these things:

▶ using *nicht and nie* to negate a verb, remembering to place it near the end of the sentence
▶ using *nicht* to precede words for emphasis
▶ using indefinite pronouns: *nirgendwo, niemand*
▶ using *kein* as a negative with nouns: *keine Ahnung*
▶ using *weder ... noch* to give two balanced negatives
▶ using *nicht nur ... sondern auch* to translate 'not only ... but also'
▶ using *nichts*.

(6) Translate into English:

1 Wir dürfen nicht vergessen, dass die kulturelle Vielfalt in Europa sehr wichtig ist.
2 Haben Sie keine Angst vor der EU!
3 Im Moment hat die EU weder einen Präsidenten noch Soldaten.
4 Wir waren noch nie in Frankreich.
5 Ich habe keine Angst, meine Identität zu verlieren.
6 Alte Menschen werden nicht mehr isoliert, sondern respektiert und geschätzt sein.
7 Die EU hat nicht nur für die Zukunft gute Ideen, sondern auch konkrete Vorschläge, wie man diese Ideen finanzieren kann.
8 Europa hat nichts zu verbergen.
9 Nicht alle EU-Mitglieder wollen den Euro.
10 Die globale Wirtschaft hat kein Vertrauen in die europäischen Politiker.

Translate into German:

11 Isn't Poland a member of the EU?
12 He had not voted.
13 You will never visit Russia.
14 The EU is no longer small.
15 I would not like to be the EU President!
16 I no longer have a passport.
17 Nothing is more certain.
18 I have not a single euro left.
19 I prefer not to take my holidays in Europe.
20 I have neither the time nor the money.

Revision of AS Grammar: word order

Word order is very important in German. You must remember the rules:

> the main verb is always the second idea
> the order of adverbs is time – manner – place
> conjunctions can change the word order: *weil, wenn* and *dass* send the verb to the end of the clause
> if a sentence begins with a subordinate clause, the subject and verb in the main clause invert to form "a verb sandwich"
> in relative clauses, the verb goes to the end of the clause (NB: relative pronouns must be used in German).

(7) **Translate into English:**

1 Natürlich hat sie sich sehr gefreut, als sie gute Noten bekommen hat.
2 Viele Frauen entscheiden sich für Teilzeitarbeit, wenn sie Kinder haben.
3 Er hat nicht viel in der Schule gearbeitet, aber jetzt arbeitet er fleißig in der Lehre.
4 Sie studiert in Deutschland, weil sie sehr gut Deutsch sprechen kann.
5 Da sie in einer Bank arbeiten will, hofft sie, Mathe an der Universität zu studieren.
6 Marlene Dietrich ist nach Amerika ausgewandert, weil sie die Nazis hasste.
7 ‚Lola rennt' ist die Geschichte einer Frau, die ihren Freund retten will.
8 Berlin ist eine schöne Stadt mit viel Geschichte.
9 Da man in der Schweiz verschiedene Sprachen spricht, ist es ein kompliziertes Land.
10 Brandenburg ist eines der neuen Bundesländer, die früher ein Teil der DDR waren.

Translate into German:

11 Last year, I studied at Bremen University.
12 Many young people speak foreign languages very well and therefore can find work anywhere in the EU.
13 She was not interested in big films but wanted to tell unusual stories.
14 Anne Frank liked it very much when people visited her.
15 The Stasi time was very difficult because you distrusted everyone.
16 The Nazi time was just as bad, as everyone was afraid.
17 As West Berliners could no longer go to East Berlin, many people could not go to work.
18 The wall was built because many East Germans wanted to leave the country.
19 West Berlin was very isolated because there was only one road in.
20 Marlene Dietrich was born in Berlin in 1901.

Grammar

A2 Grammar: the subjunctive

What you need to know

As well as an alternative to the conditional, the subjunctive in German in used for direct or reported speech. The present and perfect subjunctive are the most useful here:

To form the present subjunctive, add the following endings to the stem of the verb:

ich -e, du -est, er/sie -e, wir -en, ihr -et, sie -en.

The exception to this is *sein:*

ich sei, du seiest, er sei, wir seien, ihr seiet, sie seien.

The perfect subjunctive is formed quite logically with the present subjunctive of the auxiliary *haben* or *sein* plus the past participle: *ich sei gegangen, ich habe gemacht.*

The imperfect subjunctive is often used for politeness, expressing wishes and requests:

ich hätte gern ..., ich möchte ...

The imperfect and pluperfect subjunctives are frequently used after conjunctions such as *als* and *als ob.*

The future subjunctive is formed by using the present subjunctive of *werden* plus the infinitive.

8 Translate into English:

1 Die Studenten erklärten, sie seien immer sehr spät ins Bett gegangen.
2 Meine Freundin fragte mich, ob ich Fremdsprachen studieren wolle.
3 Er hat immer gesagt, dass ihm seine Arbeit gefalle.
4 Sie sagte, sie habe zu viel zu tun.
5 Ich möchte ein gutes Zeugnis haben.
6 Es sieht nicht so aus, als ob er Arbeit finden würde.
7 Sie tut nicht so, als wäre sie fleiβig.
8 Würden Sie bitte hier unterschreiben?
9 Ich hätte gern einen guten Job.
10 Sie sagten, sie hätten nichts geplant.

Translate into German:

11 I would like to study in Germany.
12 She said that she was happy.
13 They acted as though they loved German.
14 He said the film was really good.
15 They said they saw a wonderful play last week.
16 Would you please sit down?
17 She looked as though she was tired.
18 I said I did not want to work every day.
19 She asked why we did not come to the party.
20 It isn't as if she went out every night.

A2 Grammar: the passive

What you need to know

At A2 Level, you are expected to be familiar with the use of the passive tenses:

▶ the present passive: *es wird gemacht* = it is being done
▶ the imperfect passive: *es wurde gemacht* = it was being done
▶ the perfect passive: *es ist gemacht worden* = it has been done
▶ the pluperfect passive: *es war gemacht worden* = it had been done
▶ the future passive: *es wird gemacht werden* = it will be done

NB: with modal verbs, the tense is expressed through the modal verb, and the other verb remains in the passive infinitive: *es muss sofort gemacht werden.*

(9) Translate into English:

1 Es wurde ihnen gesagt, dass man schnell etwas tun solle.
2 In der Umweltpolitik wird nicht genug getan.
3 Abwässer von Chemiefabriken wurden oft in den Rhein geleitet.
4 Atomkraft wird in vielen Kraftwerken produziert.
5 Plastiktüten werden mehrmals verwendet.
6 Plastikflaschen wurden durch Glasflaschen ersetzt.
7 Sperrmüll wurde regelmäßig abgeholt.
8 Abfallsünder wurden bestraft.
9 Katalysatoren mussten in Autos eingebaut werden.
10 In vielen Gärten sind Komposthaufen schon angelegt worden.

Translate into German:

11 It will never be done.
12 Glass and metal were collected separately.
13 Pictures of rubbish heaps and the hole in the ozone layer are being shown.
14 Old paper had been collected.
15 Competitions with prizes were organised.
16 Wonderful cloth bags have been produced.
17 The shopping ought to be put in them.
18 The bus has been used more often.
19 The bike cannot be used at the moment.
20 It was damaged in an accident last week.

Pronunciation

b, d und g

CD Track 8

Vergleichen Sie:

Bild	o**b**
blei**b**en	schrei**b**t
Deutsch	gesun**d**
dürfen	bal**d**
gut	Ta**g**
ganz	Erfol**g**

Consonants **b**, **d** and **g** are pronounced like **p**, **t** and **k** respectively when they appear at the end of a word or in front of **s** or **t**.

Üben Sie jetzt diese Sätze:

Jeden Tag gesund essen – der gute Weg zum Erfolg!
Mein deutscher Freund wird bald kommen.
Ich weiß nicht, ob er lange bleibt.

-ig, -ich, -isch

CD Track 9

Wiederholen Sie die Adjektive:

wen**ig**	mögl**ich**	prak**tisch**
bill**ig**	eigentl**ich**	poli**tisch**
witz**ig**	jugendl**ich**	laun**isch**
güns**tig**	schriftl**ich**	erfinder**isch**

Versuchen Sie jetzt diesen Zungenbrecher:

Theoretisch ist das richtig, aber eigentlich gar nicht wichtig – beschwichtigt der ewig praktische Herr Derwisch.

s, ß, st, sp

CD Track 10

Üben Sie diese Wörter:

Sonntag	sein
Stein	Straße
Fußball	Spaß
Sorge	Pass
Staatsangehörigkeit	Statistik

Zungenbrecher:

Am Sonntag sitzt sein Sohn auf der Straße in der Stadt, sonst strickt er Socken, spielt Fußball und sammelt Steine.

ei, ie CD Track 11

Wiederholen Sie:

eins, zwei, drei
Eintracht und Zwietracht
Dienstag, Mittwoch und Freitag
schwierig
der Schweiß
Die Arbeit ist nicht schwierig, aber schweißtreibend.
Ich schreibe. Ich schrieb. Ich habe geschrieben.
Er muss sich entscheiden. Er hat sich entschieden.
Liebeslieder von Liebe und Leiden

Lange und kurze Vokale CD Track 12

Wiederholen Sie:

langer Vokal:
mag, Rad, Spaß, Abend, sagen
sehr, gehen, jedes, Federball, Meter
mir, hier, Spiel, Ziel, viel
ohne, wohnen, so, oder, Mode
Ruhe, Schule, Fuß, zu, nun

kurzer Vokal:
hallo, etwas, Geschmack, Stadt, satt
Essen, Tennis, schlecht, Welt, Geld
bist, sich, immer, finden, Wirkung
kommen, besonders, Kosten, gebrochen, noch
muss, Mutter, Eiskunstlauf, Druck, Schuss

Vokale mit Umlaut CD Track 13

Wiederholen Sie:

schön	*erhöht*	*gewöhnlich*	*könnte*
über	*hübsch*	*Grüße*	*müsste*
Ähnlichkeit	*erwähnen*	*Fähigkeit*	*ändern*

Lesen Sie diese Wörter laut. Überprüfen Sie danach die Aussprache.

übertrieben	*Aufklärungsarbeit*	*hören*	*jeder fünfte*	*Gegensätze*
möglich	*Gefühl*	*Schönheitsideal*	*schädlich*	*fünf*
Essstörungen	*gefährlich*	*Öffentlichkeit*	*übermäßig*	*abhängig*

Zungenbrecher:

Der Mondschein schien schon schön.

35

Pronunciation

-z und -zw CD Track 14

Wiederholen Sie:

Ziel	Zug	Zaun	Zweig	Zwerg	Zweck
Einzelzimmer	jetzt	zuletzt	kurz	nützlich	
Unterstützung	Sturz	Arzt	zwanzig	gezwungen	zwölf

Hören Sie zu und wiederholen Sie:

jetzt – zuletzt
zu zweit – Zeit
kurz – Sturz
zwanzig – Zwetschgen
Zweck – Zecke

Probieren Sie diese Sätze:

Setzen Sie sich in den Zug.
Zwischen zwölf und zwei.
Zieh jetzt kurz am Seil.
Zwei Ziegen sitzen vor dem Zaun.

Zungenbrecher:

Zwischen zwei Zelten zwitschern zwölf Zaunkönige.

Compound words CD Track 15

Wiederholen Sie:

a Gleich/geschlechtliche Partnerschaften
b Lebens/abschnitts/gefährte
c Wieder/heirat
d Geschäfts/reise
e auseinander/brechen
f Kinder/tages/stätte
g Wieder/vereinigung
h Gehirn/masse
i Wohn/gemeinschaft
j Abenteuer/lust

Unit 1: Umweltverschmutzung und Energieverbrauch

die Umwelt	the environment
der Umweltschutz	environmental conservation
der Treibhauseffekt	greenhouse effect
die Energiekrise	the energy crisis
der Energiebedarf	energy need
der Sonnenkollektor(-en)	a solar panel
die Sonnenenergie/der Solarstrom	solar energy
die Energiequelle	source of energy
das Windrad	wind turbine
die Atomenergie	nuclear power
das Kernkraftwerk	nuclear power station
belasten	to pollute
verpesten	to pollute
schaden	to damage
verschwenden	to waste
vergiften	to poison
gefährden	to endanger
erschöpft werden	to run out
die Entwaldung	deforestation
die Erwärmung der Erdatmosphäre	global warming
die Überschwemmung	flood
der Orkan(-e)	hurricane
schmelzen	to melt
der Säuregehalt	level of acidity
der Meeresspiegel	ocean level
die Ursache	cause
die Auswirkung	effect
der Klimawandel	climate change
der Gletscher	glacier

Unit 2: Umweltschutz

umweltfreundlich	environmentally friendly
umweltfeindlich	damaging to the environment
schützen	to protect
das Umweltbewusstsein	environmental awareness
die Umwelterziehung	environmental education
die Schadstoffbelastung mindern	to reduce damage by pollutants
retten	to save
die Bedrohung der Menschen	threat to humanity
die dauerhafte Entwicklung	sustainable development
demonstrieren/eine Demonstration	to demonstrate/a demonstration
verbessern	to improve
das Benehmen ändern	to change the behaviour

37

die Ausstellung	exhibition
kämpfen gegen	to fight against
der Gegner	activists
das Licht ausschalten	to put out the light
die Heizung herunterdrehen	to turn down the heating
die Fahrgemeinschaft	car-sharing
Müll trennen	(to separate) household rubbish
der Sperrmüll	bulky rubbish
recyceln/das Recycling	to recycle/recycling
die Industrieländer	the industrialised countries
alternative Energiequellen	alternative energy sources
entwickeln	to develop
die Plastiktüte	plastic bag
biologisch abbaubar	biodegradable
vernichten	to destroy
das Benzin	petrol
das Rohöl	crude oil
die Kohle	coal
der Energieverbrauch	energy consumption
der Brennstoff	fuel
der Wasserstoff	hydrogen
der Sauerstoff	oxygen
das Kohlendioxid	carbon dioxide CO_2

Unit 3: Ausländer

der Ausländer	foreigner
der Aussiedler	resettler
der Gastarbeiter	guest worker
der Asylbewerber	asylum seeker
das Herkunftsland	country of origin
der Einwanderer	immigrant
der Auswanderer	emigrant
der Antrag	application
verfolgt	persecuted
integrieren	integrate
der Bürger	citizen
die Einbürgerung	citizenship
die Aufenthaltserlaubnis	residence permit
die Arbeitsgenehmigung	work permit
die Familie nachholen	to bring one's family over
sich einleben	to settle down
unqualifizierte Arbeit	unskilled work
schlecht bezahlt	poorly paid
niedrig	menial

ablehnen	to reject
die kulturelle Indentität wahren	to maintain cultural identity
Anst haben (vor)	to be afraid
die Ungleichheit	inequality
der Rassismus	racism
die Rassendiskriminierung	racial discrimination
die Ausländerfeindlichkeit	xenophobia, dislike of foreigners
der Neonazismus	neo-Nazism
der kulturelle Konflikt	cultural clash
verschlimmern/verbessern	to get worse/to improve
der Sündenbock	scapegoat
die Rassenkonflikte	racial tensions
die Gewalt	violence
die Rassenunruhen	riots
die Feindseligkeit	hostility
fremd	foreign
der gegenseitige Respekt	mutual respect
die Toleranz	tolerance
die kulturelle Vielfalt	cultural diversity
zweisprachig	bilingual

Unit 4: Armut und Reichtum

die Armut	poverty
das Elend	misery
die Armutsgrenze	poverty threshold
die Kluft	gap
der Reichtum	riches
der Obdachlose	homeless person
obdachlos	homeless
arbeitslos/die Arbeitslosigkeit	unemployed/unemployment
betteln	to beg
der Bettler	beggar
die Herberge	hostel
die Dritte Welt	the Third World
die Sozialhilfe	social services
die Entwicklungsländer	developing countries
die Unterernährung	malnutrition
die Hungersnot	famine
die Dürre	drought
die Infektionskrankheiten	infectious diseases
der Krieg	war
die Katastrophe	disaster
das Erdbeben	earthquake
die medizinische Fürsorge	medical/health care

teilen	to share
Probleme lösen	to solve problems
die Ausbildung anregen	to encourage schooling
fairer Handel	fair trade
von seiner Arbeit leben	to live from one's work
die Ausbeutung	exploitation
die Biobaumwolle	organic cotton
das anständige Gehalt	fair pay
die Gleichberechtigung	equality
das Wohlwollen	goodwill
die Grundrechte	basic rights
die moralischen Werte	ethical values
der Wohlfahrtsverband	charity
fördern	(to) support
freiwillig	voluntary

Unit 5: Rechtswesen und Verbrechen

die Gewalt	violence
tatverdächtig sein	to be suspected (of a crime)
das Delikt(e)	crime
verurteilt	convicted
der Straftäter	criminal
die Straftat	crime
der Ladendiebstahl	shoplifting
die Sachbeschädigung	criminal damage
Schwarzfahren	fare dodging
die Körperverletzung	physical injury
anzeigen	to press charges
begehen	commit
benachrichtigen	to report
das Verbrechen	crime
der Diebstahl	theft
die Gewalttat	crime of violence
das Gerichtsverfahren	court hearing
der Betrug	fraud, scam
das Betäubungsmittel	narcotic
die Strafverfolgungsbehörde	law enforcement agency
erforderlich	necessary, essential
verführen	to seduce
verboten	forbidden
illegal	illegal
vorsichtig	careful
misstrauisch	suspicious

verlockend	alluring, tempting
die Gefängnisstrafe	prison sentence
das Gefängnis	prison
die Todesstrafe	death penalty
die Abschreckung	deterrent
das Opfer	victim
die Überwachungskamera	security camera

Unit 6: Technik und die Zukunft

die neue Technologie	new technology
genetisch	genetic
die Gentechnik	genetic engineering
das Klonen/klonen	cloning/to clone
entdecken	to discover
gentechnisch verändert	genetically modified
genmanipuliert	genetically modified
das Erbgut	genetic make-up
das Gen	gene
erfinden/die Erfindung	to invent/invention
die Zeitreise	time travel
die Reise begrenzen	to limit the journey
im Internet einkaufen	to shop on the Internet
der Fortschritt	progress
ein defektes Gen	a defective gene
eine erblich bedingte Fehlsteuerung	a congenital disorder
die Erbkrankheit	hereditary illness
heilen	to cure
ethische Bedenken	ethical considerations
die Transplantation	transplant
das Retortenbaby	test-tube baby
der Embryo	embryo
der DNS-Code	DNA code
der Spender	donor
die Lebensqualität	quality of life
verbessern	to improve
entwickeln	to develop
Wirklichkeit werden	to become reality
forschen über	to research into
die Forschung	research
das Reagenzglas	test tube
die embryonale Stammzelle	embryonic stem cell
ausgestorben	extinct

Unit 7: Literatur, Film und die schönen Künste

die Schönheit	beauty
die Wahrheit	truth
der Geschmack	taste
schildern	to depict
der Leser	the reader
eine Geschichte erzählen	to tell a story
in anderen Sprachen übersetzt	translated into other languages
das Drehbuch	screenplay
einen Film drehen	to make a film
der Handwerker	craftsman
der Dichter	poet
das Gedicht	poem
der Regisseur	director
der Roman	novel
der Künstler	artist
der Schriftsteller	writer
das Stück	play
der Titel	title
düster	bleak
die Hauptfigur	main character
die Regie	direction
die Anerkennung	recognition
der Kassenerfolg	box-office success
die Kritik	review
der Schauplatz	scene
der Schauspieler	actor
der Hauptdarsteller	principal actor
die Landschaft	landscape
das Mitglied	member
entdeckt	discovered
der Schwarzmarkt	black market
der Maler	painter
das Motiv	theme
das Werk	work
zu Lebzeiten	when alive
das Gemälde	painting
der Architekt	architect

Unit 8: Deutschland heute

die Mauer	wall
die Teilung	separation
die Wende	turning point

die Wiedervereinigung	reunification
Ossis	people from East Germany
Wessis	people from West Germany
die EU	European Union
der Euro	euro
die Muttersprache	mother tongue
die Wirtschaft	economy
das Wirtschaftswachstum	economic growth
das Zusammengehörigkeitsgefühl	feeling of belonging
die Mitgliedstaaten (pl)	member states
deutschsprachig	German speaking

Unit 9: Die Politik und globale Probleme

die Globalisierung	globalisation
die Regierung	government
der Staat	state
die Wirtschaftsmacht	economic power
der Weltmarkt	world market
wettbewerbsfähig	competitive
die Demokratie	democracy
die Macht	power
das Recht	the right
versammeln	to assemble, congregate
rechtsextremistisch	right-wing
der Krieg	war
der Frieden	peace
beherrschen	rule
der Angriff	attack
der Drahtzieher	manipulator
der Attentäter	assassin
der Terrorverdächtige	terrorist suspect
vereitelt	thwarted
der Bundestag	German parliament
der Eiserne Vorhang	Iron Curtain
die Ölkrise	oil crisis
der Abbau	phasing out
Terrorismus bekämpfen	to combat terrorism
stimmen für/gegen	to vote for/against
die Wahl	election
die Stimme	the vote

1

1 We must use cooler water in the washing machine.
2 Forest exploitation shows no respect for nature.
3 We expect better next time!
4 Carbon dioxide has the worst effect on our atmosphere.
5 We have no more realistic solutions.
6 What should we do to find the right road?
7 The transport system of the future will be much more efficient.
8 A varied diet is better for health.
9 I am clearly more optimistic than you are.
10 The sun is a direct source of light and heat.
11 Züge sind umweltfreundlicher als Autos.
12 Wir haben genug Erdgas, aber kein Benzin.
13 Ein altes Auto ist nicht gut für die Umwelt.
14 Ein neues Auto ist genauso schlimm wie ein altes.
15 Ihr Haus hat Sonnenkollektoren.
16 Meine Zentralheizung ist teuer.
17 Es gibt eine gute Atmosphäre im Ökodorf.
18 Dort wohnen die Leute billiger als bei uns.
19 Recyceln Sie (Recycelst du) alte Zeitungen und leere Flaschen?
20 Welche Energie ist am billigsten?

2

1 Immigrants? Do we pay them child benefit?
2 According to German law, no one can be disadvantaged because of their race.
3 Immigrants came to Germany with their families.
4 In the last hundred years, German re-settlers have suffered much because of their nationality.
5 We all have the right to the nationality of the country in which we are born.
6 Immigrants came to work in our country.
7 We stand against anyone who doesn't respect human rights.
8 Germany is the country in which I grew up and whose culture I try to adapt to.
9 I am not allowed to forget my origins.
10 We are regarded as belonging to nowhere.
11 Erklären Sie (Erkläre) mir, was Rassismus bedeutet.
12 Ich habe ihnen gesagt, dass ich sie nicht verstehe.
13 Er wohnt jetzt in Leipzig und findet die Stadt sehr ruhig.
14 Das ist eine Stadt, die ich nicht kenne.
15 Gastarbeiter sind hauptsächlichTürken, die zum Arbeiten nach Deutschland gekommen sind.
16 Die Aussiedler sind Deutsche, die jetzt in Osteuropa wohnen.
17 Sie wohnen dort seit 20 Jahren.
18 Die Karte? Zeigen Sie (Zeig) sie mir, bitte.

19 Die Ausländerfeindlichkeit – was ist die Ursache davon?
20 Wir müssen versuchen, sie mit Toleranz zu ersetzen.

1 How do you solve these problems?
2 Do you already do something to raise money for a charity?
3 What do such charities need in order to be able to function?
4 We must find a long-term solution.
5 Without a job, you cannot pay the rent.
6 Without accommodation it is difficult to find a job
7 We try to help these people to rebuild their society.
8 The Third World countries should be allowed to forget their debts to the industrial countries.
9 We must not forget that all people need help.
10 When you live in absolute poverty, you do not have enough to eat.
11 Jeder sollte einen bestimmten Lebensstandard haben.
12 Arbeitest du/Arbeiten Sie bei einer Wohlfahrtsorganisation?
13 Ich will anderen Leuten helfen, eine Zukunft zu haben.
14 In vielen Ländern können viele Leute weder schreiben noch lesen.
15 Ich hoffe, ihnen helfen zu können.
16 Sie will nach Afrika gehen, um dort den Kindern zu helfen.
17 Wir arbeiten dort schon seit zehn Jahren.
18 Das Leben kann für allein erziehende Mütter sehr schwierig sein.
19 Viele junge Leute wollen reich sein.
20 Was macht man, wenn man keinen Job finden kann?

1 The poet Johann Wolfgang von Goethe was born in 1749.
2 Karl Wilhelm Gropius trained as a landscape painter in Berlin.
3 In this era, society was dominated by men.
4 Fassbinder was born in 1945 and spent his childhood in a chaotic post-war Germany.
5 Marlene Dietrich went to school in Berlin and Dessau.
6 In April 1930, she left Germany and emigrated to America.
7 Roland Emmerich began his career as a film director in Germany.
8 Later he found fame in America.
9 Wim Wenders' first successful film was 'Paris, Texas' (1984).
10 His 1987 film 'Wings of Desire' inspired the 1998 film 'City of Angels' with Meg Ryan and Nicholas Cage.
11 Wie viele Leute haben das Pergamonmuseum im Jahr 2007 besucht?
12 Letztes Jahr wurde dieses Bild für $78 000 000 verkauft.
13 Christa Wolf wurde 1929 geboren.
14 Sie glaubte nicht an die Auflösung der DDR.
15 Lessing studierte zuerst Medizin und Theologie in Leipzig.
16 Danach lebte er als Schriftsteller in Berlin, wo er für mehrere Zeitungen schrieb.

17 1995 gewann Franka Potente den Bayerischen Filmpreis als beste Nachwuchsschauspielerin.
18 Tom Tykwer schrieb die Rolle der Lola im Film ‚Lola rennt' für sie.
19 Franka Potente hat auch ein Drehbuch geschrieben.
20 Annette von Droste-Hülshoff schrieb schöne Balladen und Gedichte über Westfalen.

1 Tomorrow we will live in a world full of computers.
2 In the future, computers will help you get everything done.
3 It will no longer be necessary to leave the house, for you will have everything you need at home.
4 Scientists' decisions will have serious consequences.
5 Because of genetics, it will be possible to cure many hereditary illnesses.
6 But there will be no miracle cure in the next five years.
7 Genetic manipulation could create a world full of perfect people.
8 All food will be genetically modified.
9 Genetically modified food could cause new allergies.
10 If you knew that such food was harmless, you could solve the food problems of the developing countries with it.
11 Wie werden wir in der Zukunft leben?
12 Es wird überall Computer geben.
13 Wir werden im Internet einkaufen.
14 Man wird seinen Urlaub auf dem Mond verbringen können.
15 Wie wird das tägliche Leben aussehen?
16 Mein Computer wird mir helfen, Entscheidungen zu treffen.
17 Die Wissenschaftler werden sehr verantwortungsvoll sein müssen.
18 Ich möchte nicht in einer perfekten Welt wohnen.
19 Man sollte mehr über Technologie wissen.
20 Wenn ich jung wäre, würde ich Informatik studieren.

1 We must not forget that cultural diversity is very important in Europe.
2 Don't be afraid of the European Union!
3 For the moment, the EU has neither president nor soldiers.
4 We have never been to France.
5 I am not afraid of losing my identity.
6 Old people will no longer be isolated but respected and valued.
7 Not only has the EU good ideas for the future but also concrete proposals to finance these ideas.
8 Europe has nothing to hide.
9 Not all EU members want the euro.
10 The global economy has no confidence in the European politicians.
11 Ist Polen kein EU-Mitglied?
12 Er hatte nicht gewählt.

13 Du wirst (Sie werden) Russland nie besuchen.
14 Die EU ist nicht mehr klein.
15 Ich möchte nicht EU-Präsident sein!
16 Ich habe keinen Pass mehr.
17 Nichts ist sicherer.
18 Ich habe keinen einzigen Euro übrig.
19 Ich verbringe meine Ferien lieber nicht in Europa.
20 Ich habe weder die Zeit noch das Geld.

1 Of course she was pleased when she got good marks.
2 Many women choose to work part-time when they have children.
3 He did not work much in school, but he works very hard now in his apprenticeship.
4 She is studying in Germany because she can speak German very well.
5 Because she wants to work in a bank, she hopes to study maths at university.
6 Marlene Dietrich emigrated to America because she hated the Nazis.
7 "Run, Lola, Run" is the story of a woman who wants to save her boyfriend.
8 Berlin is a beautiful city with lots of history.
9 Because they speak different languages in Switzerland, it is a complicated country.
10 Brandenburg is one of the new federal counties which used to be a part of the GDR.
11 Letztes Jahr habe ich an der Universität Bremen studiert.
12 Viele junge Leute sprechen sehr gut Fremdsprachen, und deshalb können sie überall in der EU einen Job finden.
13 Sie interessierte sich nicht für große Filme, sondern wollte außergewöhnliche Geschichten erzählen.
14 Es hat Anne Frank sehr gefallen, als Leute sie besucht haben.
15 Die Stasizeit war sehr schlimm, weil man jedem misstraute.
16 Die Nazizeit war genauso schlimm, da jeder Angst hatte.
17 Da die Westberliner nicht mehr nach Ostberlin durften, konnten viele Leute nicht zur Arbeit gehen.
18 Man hat die Mauer gebaut, weil viele Ostdeutschen das Land verlassen wollten.
19 Westberlin war sehr isoliert, weil es nur einen Einweg gab.
20 Marlene Dietrich wurde 1901 in Berlin geboren.

1 The students explained that they always went to bed very late.
2 My friend asked me if I wanted to study languages.
3 He always said he liked his work.

4 She said she had too much to do.
5 I would like a good report.
6 It does not look as though he will find work.
7 She does not act as if she were hardworking.
8 Would you please sign here?
9 I would like a good job.
10 They said they had nothing planned.
11 Ich möchte in Deutschland studieren.
12 Sie sagte, sie sei glücklich.
13 Sie benahmen sich, als ob sie Deutsch geliebt hätten.
14 Er sagte, der Film sei wirklich gut.
15 Sie sagten, letzte Woche hätten sie ein wunderbares Theaterstück gesehen.
16 Würden Sie sich bitte hinsetzen?
17 Sie sah aus, als ob sie müde wäre.
18 Ich sagte, ich wolle nicht jeden Tag arbeiten.
19 Sie fragte, warum wir nicht auf die Party kämen.
20 Es ist nicht so, als ob sie jeden Abend ausginge.

1 They were told that something should be done quickly.
2 Not enough is being done in environmental politics.
3 Effluents from chemical factories were often poured into the Rhine.
4 Nuclear power is produced in many power stations.
5 Plastic bags are used many times.
6 Plastic bottles were replaced by glass bottles.
7 Bulky rubbish was collected regularly.
8 Litterbugs were punished.
9 Catalytic converters had to be built into cards.
10 Compost heaps have already been set up in many gardens.
11 Es wird nie gemacht werden.
12 Glas und Metall wurden getrennt gesammelt.
13 Bilder von Müllbergen und vom Ozonloch werden gezeigt.
14 Altpapier war gesammelt worden.
15 Wettbewerbe mit Preisen wurden veranstaltet.
16 Wundervolle Stofftaschen sind hergestellt worden.
17 Die Einkäufe sollten dort hineingepackt werden.
18 Der Bus ist öfter benutzt worden.
19 Das Rad kann im Moment nicht benutzt werden.
20 Es wurde letzte Woche in einem Unfall beschädigt.